INSECTS AND MINIBEASTS

Michael Leach
and Meriel Lland

Enslow Publishing
101 W. 23rd Street
Suite 240
New York, NY 10011
USA
enslow.com

This edition published in 2020 by Enslow Publishing, LLC
101 W. 23rd Street, Suite 240, New York, NY 10011

Copyright © Arcturus Holdings Ltd 2020

Cataloging-in-Publication Data

Names: Leach, Michael. | Lland, Meriel.
Title: Insects and minibeasts / Michael Leach and Meriel Lland.
Description: New York : Enslow Publishing, 2020. | Series: Animal explorers | Includes bibliographical references
and index.
Identifiers: ISBN 9781978509870 (library bound) | ISBN 9781978509856 (pbk.) | ISBN 9781978509863 (6 pack)
Subjects: LCSH: Insects—Juvenile literature. | Invertebrates—Juvenile literature.
Classification: LCC QL467.2 L43 2020 | DDC 595.7—dc23

Printed in the United States of America

To Our Readers: We have done our best to make sure all website addresses in this book were active and appropriate
when we went to press. However, the author and the publisher have no control over and assume no liability for the
material available on those websites or on any websites they may link to. Any comments or suggestions can be sent by
email to customerservice@enslow.com.

Photo Credits:
Every attempt has been made to clear copyright. Should there be any inadvertent omission, please apply to the publisher
for rectification.

Key: b-bottom, t-top, c-center, l-left, r-right

Alamy: 4–5 (Ian Cruickshank), 8–9 (Peter Schwarz, BIA/Minden Pictures), 8bl (Piotr Naskrecki/Minden Pictures), 9cr &
31bl (Michel Gunther/Biosphoto), 10–11 (Michiel Schaap/Minden Pictures), 10tr (Thomas Marent/Minden Pictures), 13cr
(Reinhard Dirscherl), 18–19 (Paul van Hoof/Minden Pictures), 19cr (Ingrid Visser/Minden Pictures), 22–23 (Matt Cole),
24–25 (Yves Lanceau/Biosphoto), 24bl (Chien Lee/Minden Pictures), 25cr (Jaap Schelvis/Minden Pictures); Shutterstock:
cover and title page; 4cl (Puwadol Jaturawutthichai), 4br (Alen thien), 5tr (Giedrilius), 5cl (David Bokuchava), 5br
(Dennis van de Water), 6–7 (Florian Teodor), 6tr (Gmarosso), 6br (Vectorworks_Enterprise), 7cr (Jarun Tedjaem),
9br (Alastair Wallace), 10cl (Dennis van de Water), 10br (Park Ji Sun), 12–13 (Sergey Lavrentev), 12c (Anest), 12br
(Spreadthesign), 14–15 (Anatoliy Lukich), 14b & 32br (InsectWorld), 15tr (jps), 15br (Sabelskaya), 16c (Sally Wallis),
16br (foodonwhite), 17br (Kostiantyn Kravchenko), 18b (aaabbbccc), 19br (Oga 77), 20–21 (schankz), 20cr (Jaroslav
Monchak), 20bl (CK Ma), 20br (ScubaPonnie), 21br (Spreadthesign), 22bl (nikjuzaili), 23tl & 31br (Bachkova Natalia),
23br (barkarola), 25br (Chalintra B), 26bl (reptiles4all), 26br (GR Photo), 27tl (Silvan Reiser), 27tr (J. A. Dunbar), 27br
(RK008), 27bl (nechaevkon), 28bl (Milan Zygmunt), 29tr (Maria Dryfhout), 29bl (photographyfirm); Wikimedia Commons:
26tr (Huber, J.T.), 26tl (Petra & Wilfried), 26cr (Alexey Polilov), 27cl (Bruno C. Vellutini).

CONTENTS

Introduction

An animal is a living organism made up of cells. It feeds, senses, and responds to its surroundings, moves, and reproduces. Scientists have identified nearly nine million species of living animals, but there are many more to be found.

Life Appears

Single-celled life forms appeared around four billion years ago. Sponges—the first animals—appeared a billion years ago. Over time, more complicated animals evolved and some also became extinct. Dinosaurs were the dominant land animals for 165 million years before they died out 65 million years ago.

Fossilized skull of the dinosaur *Tyrannosaurus rex*

Rhinoceros hornbills are birds that live in Southeast Asian rain forests. Birds are warm-blooded animals with backbones. They have wings and most can fly.

Leaf beetle, an insect

Classifying Life

Scientists organize living things into groups with shared characteristics. The two main kinds of animal are ones with backbones (vertebrates) and ones without (invertebrates). Arthropods make up the biggest invertebrate group. They have segmented bodies and jointed limbs. Insects, spiders, and crabs are all arthropods.

Warm- and Cold-Blooded

Most animals are ectothermic, or "cold-blooded." Their body temperature is controlled by their environment. Mammals and birds are endothermic, or "warm-blooded." Their bodies can generate their own heat, so they can survive in much colder habitats.

Musk ox, a mammal

Langurs in a city

Fragile Earth

We are lucky to share our world with an extraordinary richness of animals. It is important to protect our wildlife. When humans pollute or damage the environment, we harm both animals and people. The future is in our hands.

Animal Habitats

The place where an animal lives is called its habitat. Animals have evolved to inhabit just about every environment on Earth, from tropical rain forests and coral reefs to deserts, mountaintops, and ice floes. They even survive in cities.

Giant leaf–tailed gecko, vulnerable because of habitat loss

5

Minibeasts

Minibeasts are small invertebrates. They include 900,000 known insect species, as well as arachnids, such as spiders and scorpions, millipedes and centipedes, and worms. Some mollusks and crustaceans also count as minibeasts.

Count the Legs!

The word "insect" means "cut into pieces," and an adult insect always has three parts to its body—head, thorax, and abdomen. It also always has six legs in its adult form. A creepy-crawly with more or less than six legs is not an insect. Insects often have wings, but not always.

The wood louse belongs to the same family as crabs and lobsters. It is a crustacean.

PRAYING MANTIS

MANTIS RELIGIOSA

Habitat: Fields, woods, grasslands; South Asia, Southern Europe, North America, Australia
Length: Male 2.4 inches (6 cm); female 3 inches (7.5 cm)
Weight: Male 0.09 ounces (2.5 g); female 0.11 ounces (3 g)
Diet: Insects, mantids, other invertebrates
Life span: Up to 9 months
Wild population: Unknown; Least Concern

The praying mantis shoots out its front legs to grasp insect prey, such as grasshoppers and crickets.

Recycling Machines

Minibeasts that eat dead plants and animals are known as detritivores. Earthworms, millipedes, slugs, and wood lice are all detritivores. They do a useful job in the food chain because they reuse nutrients, so these do not go to waste.

The shocking pink dragon millipede eats rotting leaves. It protects itself from predators by producing cyanide, a deadly poison.

The long body can be green, yellow, brown, or even black. It has two pairs of wings. Females cannot fly with their wings, but males can.

Spiders and Scorpions

A crab spider has eight eyes to see in all directions. It lies in wait, perfectly disguised, ready to ambush insect visitors to the flower.

Along with mites and ticks, scorpions and spiders are arachnids. There are at least 45,700 species of spiders and 1,750 kinds of scorpions. They are eight-legged predators with no antennae or wings. All scorpions and most spiders have venom, but few are fatal to humans.

Super Spiders

All spiders spin silk, but not all build webs. From spiral orbs to tubes and funnels, spider webs are used to trap prey. Other spiders have different hunting methods. The trapdoor spider ambushes prey from a hidden lair, while the huntsman chases its prey. Spiders range in size from a pinhead-sized orbweb to the massive goliath tarantula.

The two front walking legs are also used to grasp bees, flies, and other prey.

The world's biggest spider, the goliath tarantula, can weigh 6.2 ounces (175 g). It hunts mice, lizards, and small birds.

There are more than 2,000 species of crab spider. Many match the flowers where they hunt for insect prey each day.

The leg-like pedipalps on either side of the jaws crush and tear up food.

Sting in the Tail

While spiders inject venom with their fangs, the scorpion produces venom from a stinger at the end of its curving tail. It stings to protect itself from predators. It can also stun struggling prey, but usually it saves its venom and kills prey with its powerful pincers.

Scorpions are tough survivors, found in many harsh habitats. This yellow fattail scorpion lives in deserts in North Africa and the Middle East.

CRAB SPIDER

THOMISUS ONUSTUS

Habitat: Moors, deserts, grasslands; Europe, Asia, Africa
Length: Male 0.16 inches (4 mm); female 0.28 inches (7 mm)
Weight: Male 0.09 ounces (2.5 g); female 0.11 ounces (3 g)
Diet: Small invertebrates
Life span: Up to 4 months
Wild population: Unknown

Beetles

A stag beetle lives just a few months as an adult. It spends up to six years as a larva, eating rotting wood.

A quarter of all the species on Earth are beetles. There are about 400,000 known species. These insects have two pairs of wings, but only the back pair is used for flight. The hard front pair acts as a protective shell. Beetles have four stages in their life cycle: egg, larva (grub), pupa, and adult.

Beetle Diets

Most beetles are plant eaters, but some are hunters. Fast-moving tiger beetles chase their prey. Most ladybugs consume aphids or scale insects. Ground beetles feed on maggots, worms, grubs, snails, and slugs. Dung beetles specialize in animal dung.

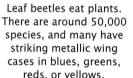

The giraffe weevil, named for its long neck, lives in Madagascar. It feeds on the leaves of a tree known as the giraffe beetle tree.

Leaf beetles eat plants. There are around 50,000 species, and many have striking metallic wing cases in blues, greens, reds, or yellows.

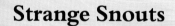

Strange Snouts

Weevils are the largest beetle family, with more than 60,000 species. They are plant eaters and have an especially long snout. Most weevils specialize in eating a particular kind of leaf, flower, fruit, seed, grain, or nut.

STAG BEETLE

LUCANUS CERVUS

Habitat: Hills, mountains; Europe, Asia, Africa
Length: Male 2.8 in (7 cm); female 1.6 in (4 cm)
Weight: Male 0.14 oz (4 g); female 0.09 oz (2.5 g)
Diet: Larvae: rotting wood; adults: nectar, tree sap
Life span: Up to 6 years
Wild population: Unknown; Near Threatened

Male stag beetles wrestle each other with "antlers" (modified jaws). The winner will mate with the female.

Sensitive antennae pick up vibrations, smells, and tastes. The beetle cleans its antennae regularly with its front legs.

Each of the stag beetle's six legs ends in a claw used for climbing and gripping.

The beetle's wing case is called an elytra. It forms a tough shell that protects against predators.

Slugs and Snails

Slugs and snails are gastropods, a kind of mollusk. There are around 75,000 species, and a third of these live on land. The others live in the oceans and in fresh water. Slugs and snails are found worldwide except in places of extreme cold. They have soft, slimy bodies and they move along slowly on a single, broad foot.

The spiral shell, made mostly of chalk, protects the snail from birds and other predators.

Almost the Same

Snails have a protective shell, but slugs do not. Slugs squeeze under logs or stones to stay safe and moist. Apart from that, slugs and snails are very similar. They feed mostly on plants and move slowly along a slime trail. They are also both hermaphrodites (part male and part female), so when they mate, each partner lays eggs.

The leopard slug eats dead plants and fungi, but also hunts other slugs.

COMMON GARDEN SNAIL

CORNU ASPERSUM "SPECKLED HORN"

Habitat: Gardens, farmland, meadows, forests; Europe, Asia, North Africa
Shell width: 1.4 inches (3.5 cm)
Weight: 1 ounce (30 g)
Diet: Plants
Life span: Up to 2 years
Wild population: Unknown; Least Concern

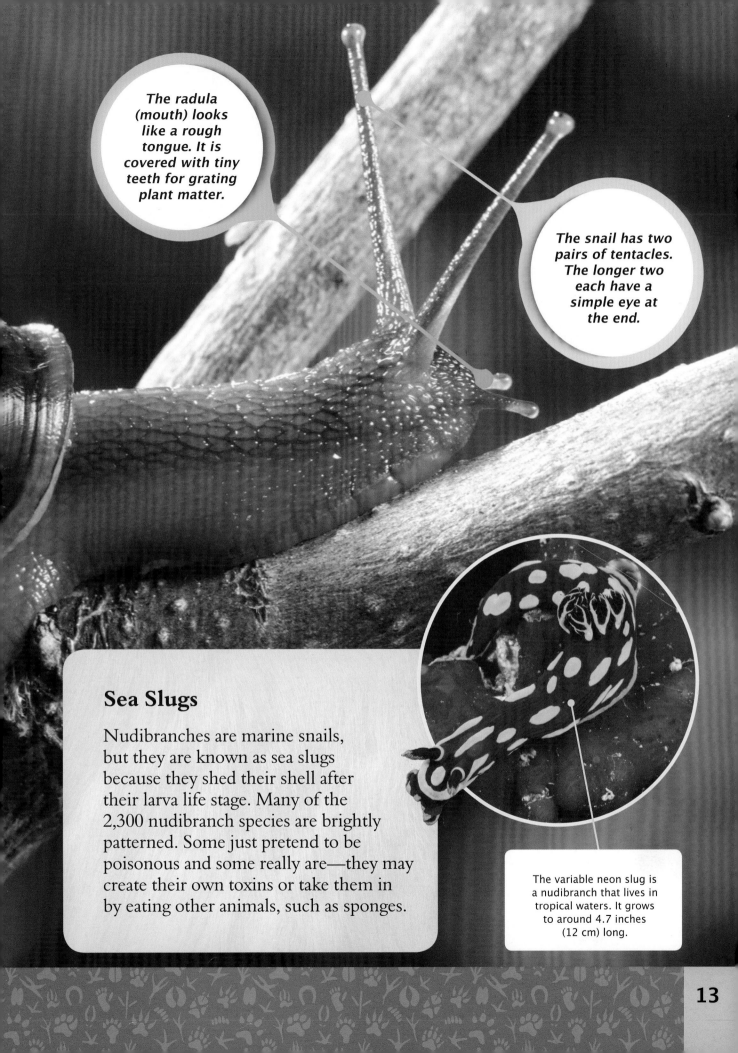

The radula (mouth) looks like a rough tongue. It is covered with tiny teeth for grating plant matter.

The snail has two pairs of tentacles. The longer two each have a simple eye at the end.

Sea Slugs

Nudibranches are marine snails, but they are known as sea slugs because they shed their shell after their larva life stage. Many of the 2,300 nudibranch species are brightly patterned. Some just pretend to be poisonous and some really are—they may create their own toxins or take them in by eating other animals, such as sponges.

The variable neon slug is a nudibranch that lives in tropical waters. It grows to around 4.7 inches (12 cm) long.

Butterflies

Butterflies and moths are insects that feed on sweet, sugary nectar or fruit juice. There are about 180,000 species. Most moths are active at night and their wings are duller. Butterflies fly by day. Their antennae (feelers) are thin with a rounded end, while moths' antennae are feathery along their whole length.

Millions of monarch butterflies spend winter in Mexico. They roost in fir trees.

Wonderful Wings

The wings of butterflies and moths are made of a hardened protein called chitin. They are covered with thousands of overlapping, powdery scales, so small they can only be seen under a microscope. The scales can be bright reds, oranges, yellows, or blues—all hues that help them to attract a mate or ward off predators. Others create mottled patterns that help the butterfly or moth to blend in with the background.

Swallowtails are named for their forked back wings. There are more than 550 species. This common yellowtail swallowtail is found across the northern hemisphere.

Monarch butterflies fly up to 3,000 miles (4,750 km) a year, migrating to and from their winter roost sites.

Adult butterflies sip nectar through tube-like mouthparts called a proboscis. When not in use, the proboscis coils under the head.

Adult monarchs are orange and black. They contain toxins from the milkweed plants they ate as caterpillars. Monarch caterpillars are yellow, black, and white.

Complete Metamorphosis

The eggs of butterflies and moths hatch into worm-like eating machines called caterpillars. A growing caterpillar splits its skin several times—each stage is called an instar. At full size, the caterpillar's body hardens into a shell-like pupa. Inside this shell, it breaks down and rebuilds itself. Then the pupa splits and the winged adult emerges.

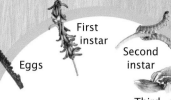

The different stages in a Kentish glory moth's life

First instar

Second instar

Eggs

Third instar

Adult female

Pupa

Adult male

Like all insects, a butterfly does not have lungs. It takes in oxygen through "spiracles"—little holes on its thorax and abdomen.

MONARCH BUTTERFLY

DANAUS PLEXIPPUS

Habitat: Woods, gardens; North and Central America, Australia, Southeast Asia
Wingspan: 3.9 inches (10 cm)
Weight: 0.02 ounces (0.5 g)
Diet: Larvae: milkweed; adults: nectar
Life span: Up to 8 weeks (6–9 months for ones that migrate)
Wild population: More than 100 million; Secure

Bees

Worldwide, excluding Antarctica, there are about 20,000 bee species. Most live alone, but honeybees and bumblebees form large colonies, made up of a queen bee, hundreds of drones, and thousands of workers. The drones mate with the queen. The workers guard the nest, collect pollen and nectar, and care for young.

Each leg is split into segments, so it is very flexible.

The bee has a pair of jointed antennae. They can touch, smell, taste, and pick up vibrations.

Breaking Away

When a bee colony becomes too large, the queen bee lays eggs that will develop into queens instead of worker bees. She leaves the nest with a large group of workers. The swarm flies to a suitable site to start a new colony. When they get there, the queen starts laying eggs already fertilized by the drones.

A swarm can contain hundreds or even thousands of honeybees.

The bumblebee has two pairs of wings. They beat up and down so quickly that they make a buzzing noise.

GARDEN BUMBLEBEE

BOMBUS HORTORUM
"PLANT BUZZER"

Habitat: Grasslands, farmland; Europe, Asia, New Zealand
Length: 0.6 inches (1.5 cm); queen 0.8 inches (2 cm)
Weight: 0.09 ounces (2.5 g); queen 0.14 ounces (4 g)
Diet: Nectar, pollen
Life span: Up to 2 weeks; queen up to 1 year
Wild population: Unknown; Least Concern

Many plants need bees to pollinate them so that they can produce fruit.

Female bumblebees can sting. Their sting is not barbed like a honeybee's, so it can be reused many times.

Finding Food

Honeybees carry nectar and pollen back to the hive. They mix nectar with saliva to make honey to feed the young. When bees find a good source of nectar, they tell the other workers where it is with an elaborate, waggling dance.

The hairy body picks up grains of pollen, which rub off on the next flower the bee visits. This is called pollination.

Bees store honey in hexagonal cells, which they build from beeswax. The cells also house eggs and larvae.

The Grasshopper Family

Grasshoppers, locusts, and crickets belong to a group of insects called orthopterans ("straight wings"). There are at least 20,000 species, and more than half are grasshoppers. Orthopterans produce sounds by rubbing together their wings or legs. They have powerful back legs for jumping.

Searching for Food

Grasshoppers are active during the day and eat plants, while crickets come out at night and are omnivores. Grasshoppers are usually solitary but sometimes they band together in great swarms, usually when rains come and end a drought. Swarming grasshoppers turn from green to yellow and black. They are known as locusts.

There can be as many as 80 million locusts in an average swarm, and they eat their own weight in plants every day.

With its long back legs, this cricket is able to jump a distance of about 3 feet (91 cm).

18

Weird Wetas

Wetas are close relatives of crickets and are found only in New Zealand. There are more than 100 species, including tree wetas, giant wetas, ground wetas, tusked wetas, and cave wetas. Many do not have wings and none of them can fly. They hide during the day and feed at night.

The cricket's antennae are much longer compared to its body length than a grasshopper's.

The Mount Arthur giant weta is heavier than a mouse. There are ten other giant weta species across New Zealand.

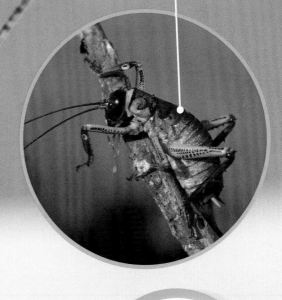

The cricket's palps taste food and pass it back into the mouth.

The cricket's ear, or tympanum, is on its front leg. (In grasshoppers, the tympanum is on the abdomen near the back legs.)

SHORT-WINGED CONEHEAD

CONOCEPHALUS DORSALIS

Habitat: Salt marshes, swamps, riverbanks, grasslands, farmland; Europe
Length: 0.6 inches (15 mm)
Weight: Male 0.09 ounces (2.5 g); female 0.14 ounces (4 g)
Diet: Grass (seeds, buds, flowers)
Life span: Up to 1 year
Wild population: Unknown; Near Threatened

Worms and Leeches

Worms are invertebrates with long, thin bodies and no limbs. There are four families: ribbon worms, roundworms, flatworms, and segmented worms. There are more than 17,000 species of segmented worms, including all the rag worms, earthworms, and leeches.

Damp Environments

Worms and leeches need to stay moist so they do not dry out. Leeches live in lakes, rivers, and wetlands. Earthworms live in the soil. They keep soil in good condition and recycle leaves and other plants by eating them and producing rich droppings.

Freaky Flatworms

Tapeworms and other flatworms are the simplest worms. They do not have an anus so they use their mouth to get rid of waste as well as take in food. They move by gliding on small body hairs. Marine flatworms can also swim by rippling their body.

Each segment is covered with tiny bristles that help the worm to move and burrow.

Most leech species are predators that hunt other invertebrates. Some, such as this medicinal leech, feed on blood. They have a sucker at each end of their body.

The tunnels that earthworms make let oxygen and rainwater into the soil.

The harmless purple flatworm (right) mimics a poisonous sea slug (left). It tricks predators into leaving it alone.

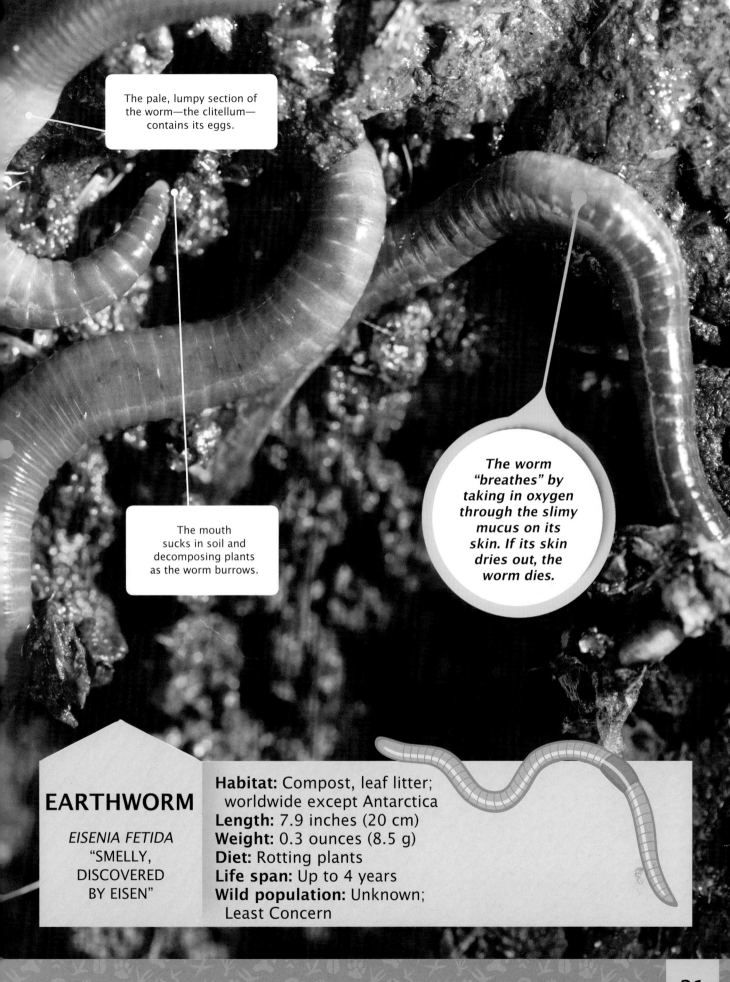

The pale, lumpy section of the worm—the clitellum—contains its eggs.

The mouth sucks in soil and decomposing plants as the worm burrows.

The worm "breathes" by taking in oxygen through the slimy mucus on its skin. If its skin dries out, the worm dies.

EARTHWORM

EISENIA FETIDA
"SMELLY, DISCOVERED BY EISEN"

Habitat: Compost, leaf litter; worldwide except Antarctica
Length: 7.9 inches (20 cm)
Weight: 0.3 ounces (8.5 g)
Diet: Rotting plants
Life span: Up to 4 years
Wild population: Unknown; Least Concern

Ants

Ants are social insects that live in colonies. Each ant has its own job. The queen lays the eggs. Workers (smaller females) collect food and look after the nest. Some species have soldiers—larger workers that protect and expand the colony. The male ants' job is to mate with the queen. There are 22,000 ant species worldwide.

Weight Lifters

Ants are omnivores. Workers find insects, seeds, nectar, and fruit to carry back to the colony. Army ants even transport much larger animals, such as lizards, scorpions, and small birds.

The antennae can pick up chemical messages called pheromones produced by other ants.

For their size, ants are the world's strongest animals. Wingless worker ants can carry more than 50 times their own body weight.

Two mandibles (jaws) at the front of the mouth can crush, slice, and bite. They move sideways, not up and down like human jaws.

Aphid Farms

Ants "farm" herds of aphids for their sugary honeydew. They stop the aphids escaping by biting off their wings or releasing chemicals that make aphids sleepy. The ants stroke the aphids' abdomens to make them ooze honeydew. The aphids also benefit because the ants fight off any predators.

This red ant is "milking" an aphid for its honeydew. Keeping aphid farms gives ants a ready supply of energy-rich food.

The ant can squirt acid from a gland at the end of the abdomen.

Ants do not have ears. A special organ near the knee makes sense of vibrations picked up from the ground by the feet.

Worker ants do not have wings. Only young queens and males have these so that they can fly away to mate.

BLACK GARDEN ANT

LASIUS NIGER

Habitat: Gardens, parks, cities; Europe, North America, Asia
Length: 0.2 inches (4 mm); queen 0.4 inches (9 mm)
Weight: 0.00004 ounces (1 mg); queen 0.0004 ounces (12 mg)
Diet: Nectar, small invertebrates, ripe fruit, human food
Life span: Up to 2 years; queen up to 20 years
Wild population: Unknown; Least Concern

Parasites

Many parasites are minibeasts, but not all. The sea lamprey is an eel–like fish that sucks the blood of other fish.

A parasite is any animal that lives on or inside another animal. Many parasites spend their entire life inside a host, while others feed off the hosts occasionally. Usually parasites do not kill their host, because then they would lose their source of food.

Outside In, or Inside Out

Many animals have parasitic worms. Tiny eggs laid in food or water enter the animal's body when it eats or drinks. The worms hatch in the intestines and live there. Parasitic wasps take no chances and lay their eggs inside a host. When the larvae hatch, they eat their host alive.

This host caterpillar is guarding fuzzy wasp pupae. The wasp larvae programmed it to do this by releasing special chemicals as they fed on its insides.

Hundreds of tiny teeth grip onto the host's flesh, while the tongue laps up blood.

Lamprey saliva contains a substance that stops blood clotting. This make its "meal" flow better.

Adaptable Fleas

Fleas are parasitic insects that use their amazing jumping power to move from one host to another. They feed on mammals' blood and their flat body is the perfect shape to move through hair or fur.

The cat flea is the most common of the 2,000 flea species. Despite its name it also sucks blood from dogs, foxes, raccoons, and skunks.

Sea lampreys are primitive fish. Like sharks, their bodies are supported by cartilage, not bone.

MALARIA MOSQUITO

ANOPHELES ALBIMANUS "WHITE-HANDED AND USELESS"

Habitat: Close to water; Central and South America
Length: 0.2 inches (6 mm)
Weight: 0.00009 ounces (2.5 mg)
Diet: Larvae: water plants; adult males: nectar; adult females: blood
Life span: Male 2 weeks; female 4 weeks
Wild population: Unknown; Least Concern

Fun Facts

Now that you have discovered lots about different kinds of minibeasts, boost your knowledge further with these 10 quick facts!

The smallest insect, a fairyfly, is smaller than a comma. It is a kind of parasitic wasp, and the female lays her tiny eggs inside other insects' eggs.

The giant huntsman has the largest leg span of any spider. At 1 foot (30 cm) across, it is larger than most dinner plates.

The world's smallest beetle is called Scydosella. It feeds on fungus and is no bigger than a grain of salt.

The African giant snail is the largest land-living gastropod. It is usually 7 inches (18 cm) long and 3.5 inches (9 cm) wide but can grow much bigger.

Queen Alexandra's birdwing is the world's largest butterfly. Females have a 9.8-inch (25 cm) wingspan. They live only in the forests of Papua New Guinea.

A healthy queen bee can lay as many as 2,000 eggs a day.

The biggest-ever swarm of locusts was in the American Midwest in 1875. It covered an area of 198,000 square miles (510,000 sq km).

The bootlace worm is a very long ribbon worm in shallow seas. One that washed ashore in 1864 was a record-breaking 180 feet (55 m).

Scientists believe that there are one million ants for every human. The world population of ants weighs more than the world population of humans.

The mosquito is the world's deadliest animal. Only females suck blood and pass on malaria, but they cause one million human deaths a year.

Your Questions Answered

We know an incredible amount about the creatures that populate our planet—from the deepest oceans to the highest mountains. But there is always more to discover. Scientists are continuing to find out fascinating details about the lives of insects and minibeasts, from their life cycles and migrations to how they hunt and survive. Here are some questions that can help you discover more about these amazing creatures.

How does the goliath tarantula catch its prey?

Often called the goliath bird-eating tarantula, this arachnid is not only huge, it can also tackle prey that is not much smaller than itself. It usually strikes from a hiding place. This is called an ambush, taking prey by surprise rather than giving chase. The goliath tarantula swiftly attacks its prey with its inch-long fangs, injecting a venom that paralyzes its victim. It then drags the prey back to its lair, where it regurgitates digestive juices, spreads them on the animal, and then sucks up the softened tissue through its straw-shaped mouth.

Goliath bird-eating tarantulas don't actually prey on birds very often; they mostly eat mice, frogs, and lizards.

How do snail shells grow?

When snails hatch from their eggs, they already have a shell. It looks different from the adult version, though, as it is still very small and very soft. Now the baby snail needs to eat a lot of calcium (the material the shell is made from) to harden and grow its shell. It starts by eating the remains of its own egg. As the snail grows, so does the shell. The baby shell remains as the innermost coils, and more and more shell is added, making the shell spiral larger. It is possible to tell the age of a snail from the number of coils in its shell—a bit like the rings of a tree trunk.

How long does it take for a caterpillar to become a butterfly?

The life cycle of a butterfly from egg to fully-developed adult can vary in length. It depends on the type of butterfly, and often also on the temperature of the environment—cold weather slows the process down, hot weather speeds it up. For example, monarch butterflies living in New Zealand take about four weeks in the summer to develop from caterpillar to butterfly. It takes about 5 to 10 days for the eggs to grow and hatch; the young animal remains a caterpillar for up to 14 days; it then cocoons itself for a further 14 days, before the butterfly hatches.

Monarch butterflies that live in North America often migrate 1,000–2,000 miles (1,600–3,200 km) every year.

Why are bees so important for humans?

In recent years, bee numbers have gone down drastically due to environmental factors such as pesticides, habitat loss, and disease. But if bees disappear, humans will be affected in many ways—bees not only pollinate many of the plants that produce our fruit and vegetables, but also those that our livestock eat. In addition, they produce wax and honey, both of which are important products for humans, too.

How do worms reproduce?

Because earthworms are hermaphrodites, they each produce sperm and eggs. This also means that, after mating, both worms will potentially end up with fertilized eggs which they place in a slimy cocoon. Each worm lays between four and 20 eggs, which hatch after about two to three weeks. As this cycle can repeat itself every week to 10 days, earthworms can multiply very quickly!

Depending on its size, an earthworm population can double in a very short space of time.

Glossary

abdomen The rear section of an insect's body.

antenna (plural antennae) One of a pair of sensory feelers on an invertebrate's head.

arthropod An invertebrate with jointed legs, a segmented body, and an exoskeleton.

crustacean An arthropod with two-part legs and a hard shell.

detritivore An animal that eats decaying plants and animals.

elytra A beetle's hard wing case.

gastropod A large mollusk, such as a snail or slug.

hermaphrodite An animal that is both male and female.

insect An animal who, in its adult form, has a body with three parts, six legs, and often wings.

invertebrate An animal that has no backbone.

larva (plural larvae) The young stage of an invertebrate that looks different from the adult.

mandible The moving mouthparts of an invertebrate.

metamorphosis The change from one form to another.

mollusk An invertebrate with a soft, unsegmented body that lives in water or damp habitats. Many mollusks have an external shell.

omnivore An animal that eats plants and meat.

pedipalp Pincer-like appendages located at the front end of many arachnids.

predator An animal that hunts and eats other animals.

prey An animal that is hunted and eaten by other animals for food.

proboscis A sucking nose or mouthpart, often tube-like, that takes up food and water.

pupa (plural pupae) An invertebrate in a hard casing that is changing from a larva to an adult. Pupae do not move.

radula A mollusk's tiny teeth, used for scraping food particles off surfaces and transporting them to the mouth.

thorax The middle section of an insect's body.

toxin A substance that can harm or kill a living being.

venom A chemical that is injected into another animal to paralyze or kill.

Further Information

BOOKS

Dussling, Jennifer. *Bugs! Bugs! Bugs!* New York, NY: DK Children's, 2011.

Mound, Laurence. *Insect.* New York, NY: DK Children's, 2017.

Murawski, Darlyne, and Nancy Honovich. *Ultimate Bug-opedia: The Most Complete Bug Reference Ever.* Washington, DC: National Geographic Kids, 2013.

Richards, Jon, and Ed Simkins. *The Natural World.* New York, NY: Crabtree Publishing, 2015.

Spelman, Lucy. *Animal Encyclopedia: 2,500 Animals with Photos, Maps, and More!* Washington, DC: National Geographic Kids, 2012.

WEBSITES

Ducksters: Insects and Arachnids
www.ducksters.com/animals/bugs.php
Head to this website to find out all about different kinds of minibeasts.

Natural History Museum: Insects
www.nhm.ac.uk/discover/insects.html
This webpage offers lots of video clips and the latest news about insects from around the world.

Index